APPLE TV 4K | HD USER GUIDE

Complete Tips and Tricks to Operate Your Apple TV Like A Pro Using Siri Remote

(Bonus: List of Siri Commands)

Tech Reviewer

@2019 Copyright

TABLE OF CONTENT

How to Use this Book

Welcome! Thank you for purchasing this book and trusting us to lead you right in operating your Apple TV device. Be rest assured that you have the right book as I have owned the Apple TV 4K for some time now and I have explored every possible tips and tricks in the book which is what I compiled to give you this detailed user guide with most current tips and tricks in the Apple TV 4K.

To better understand how the book is structured, I would advise you first read from page to page after which you can then navigate to particular sections as well as make reference to a topic individually. This book has been written in the simplest form to ensure that every user understands and gets the best out of this book. You can also use the well outlined table of content to find specific topics faster and more efficiently.

Introduction

The Apple TV was first introduced in 2015 as the fourth generation Apple TV, what is now known as the Apple TV HD. While it was seen as a fairly basic streaming box, however, it was the first to support tvOS, an OS that allows you to download apps from 3rd party developers to use on your big screen TV. The Apple TV 4k was then reintroduced. Although it has same design as the Apple TV HD, but it has lots of features stored in it. The top on the feature is the Apple A10X system on a chip used to support the 4K video of this model. Apart from the 4K support, the device also supports HDR contents through both the Dolby vision and HDR10 formats with plenty of iTunes and 3rd party contents available.

Apple launched the Apple TV 4K in response to the other 4k streaming devices that were competitive against it like the Google chrome, Amazon Fire TV and Roku. While it had its own share of rough beginning starting with the problem of the device getting stuck in the HDR mode, however, the company was able to correct this with the release of the tvOS 11.2.

The Apple TV 4k has a beautiful look, bright screens and high resolution. For every content you want to view with the Apple TV 4k, the TV would show you whether that content has 4K with HDR available which you may not see with some other competitors. You would also get several reviews for movies and TV shows spooled from several outlets like Rotten Tomatoes. You can also click on the author's profile picture to know more about the crew and casts for your favorite shows.

Thanks to the A10X fusion processor in the Apple TV, speed is guaranteed as long as your internet connection is strong, once you click on info screens, they appear immediately and you can scroll through a long list of titles at an amazing speed.

User Experience

Apple has always been particular about user experience which resulted in the catchphrases like "it just works". Apple products are usually very simple and easy for everyone to use. Apart from the richness of the TV in UX, it is convenient and contains lots of useful apps that you would enjoy.

Third Party Controllers and Accessories

If you are not pleased with the Siri Remote, you can also make use of several different accessories. Universal remotes like the ones from Caavo and Logitech can work with the Apple TV as well as the 3rd party Made-for-iPhone game controllers. To get a more personal listening experience, you can connect your Bluetooth headphones the Apple's Air pods and also connect a Bluetooth keyboard for a better typing experience. You can connect a maximum of 2 Bluetooth devices at the same time to your Apple TV. With this, you can have either a game controller and a Bluetooth headphone or have two 3rd party game controllers connected. You can also use your iPod, iPad or iPhone as an auxiliary controller for apps that supports them on your Apple TV.

Getting Started

What is in the Box

- The Apple TV itself
- Siri remote control
- USB-to-Lighting cable
- Power cable
- A small user guide

Things you need to Setup

- An Ethernet cable (if you are not using Wi-fi)
- Strong internet connection (at least 20 to 25 Mbps)

- HDMI cable, 2.0 is most recommended for Apple TV 4K. You need two cables if you want to connect to a soundbar or an A/V receiver first.
- An iOS device like an iPad or iPhone (optional)

Steps to Setup the Apple TV

You can either set up your device manually or with the iOS device. First, I would show you the general way of setting up your device, then you would see specific steps to set up your TV with a device and steps to set it up manually.

Step 1: Unbox the Apple TV and confirm that you have all the items complete.

Step 2: Insert the small end of the power cable into its appropriate space at the back of your TV while the other end goes into a power bar or wall socket. If you want to connect straight to a TV, use the HDMI cable to connect the Apple TV to your Television. If you are connecting to a A/V receiver or sound bar, use the open HDMI input on your A/V receiver to connect your Apple TV while you get a second HDMI cable to link your TV with the receiver. For a direct connection to your router, plug one end of the cable into your router and the other end into the Ethernet port of the Apple TV.

Step 3: switch on your TV and set the input selection to the same HDMI port you connected your Apple TV to. If using a receiver, ensure that the TV and the receiver are both set to their correct inputs respectively. If all is connected well, you should see the setup screen.

Step 4: Take the Siri remote control and tap the touch surface of the remote once to pair it with your Apple TV. If the remote does not connect, press the **Menu and Volume Up** buttons and hold for five seconds. If you receive a message that says you are not close enough, simply place your remote directly on your Apple TV box.

Step 5: use the touch surface of the remote to swipe down or up with your finger or thumb and choose your country (region) and language. Click on the touch surface to select your choice. If you make an error, press the menu button to return to the previous screen and attempt it again. When asked, confirm whether you would want to use Siri or not. You can always change this after setup is completed.

Step 6: if you have an iOS device like the iPad or iPhone, you can choose to transfer its settings to your Apple TV. The transfer would include things like login information for iCloud, iTunes and Wi-fi. To do this, click on **Set up with device** option and then follow the instructions that would show up on both your Apple TV and the iOS device. If you would rather not transfer settings from your iOS device or you do not have an iOS device, use the menu button of your remote to return to the previous screen and select **Set up Manually.** On

the next screens, you would have to select your
Wi-fi network, input your password and so on.

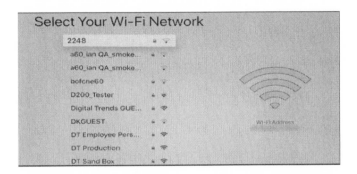

Step 7: if you have a cable subscription, you can
login to that account to watch movies and TV
shows on the Apple TV from apps that are
covered in your cable subscription. If you
purchased the Apple TV from your cable provider,
it would have been authorized already. Skip this
step if you do not have a cable subscription.

Step 8: if you have more than one Apple TV, you should make use of the **One Home Screen**. This handy feature keeps your Home screens and apps to be same across all your Apple TV devices by signing into iCloud. A message would prompt on your screen asking if you want to use One Home Screen. When you see this message, select **Match home screens.** You can decide to do this Setup later. Simply visit **Settings,** then click on **Accounts,** select **iCloud** and then choose **One Home Screen.**

Step 9: on the next screen, you would be prompted to select a room that best states where you would place the Apple TV and this would be automatically added to the Home app of any Mac computers you may have as well as your iOS devices. With this setting, you would see the Apple TV in the list of available devices in your Mac or iOS device. This feature also makes it easier for you to play music all over your home.

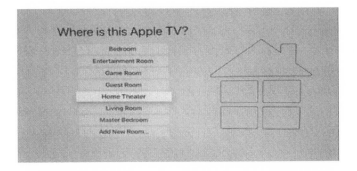

Step 10: The system would then prompt you to run through some tests to confirm that things like the Dolby Vision and HDR are working properly. And your device is set up.

How to Set Up Your Apple TV with your iPhone

There are two ways to set up your new Apple TV; either manually or with a device. We have talked about the general steps to set up your device.

Here, you would find a step by step guide to set up your device using a Device. If you have an iPod touch, iPad or the iPhone, you can set up using the **Set Up with Device** option.

Follow the steps below to do this. You would need your Siri remote to do this.

- Click the Siri remote trackpad to pair it with your TV.
- Choose your preferred **Language** from the list.
- Select your current **Country.**
- Select whether or not you want to use Siri.
- Then click on **Set Up with Device.**

- Go to your iOS device and click on **Set Up.**

- Type in the authentication code shown on your Apple TV into the field displayed on your iOS device.
- The setup process would begin.
- Go to your iOS device and tap **Done** when you see the note **Finish** on the Apple TV.
- Select when you would like the system to request for a **Password** after making purchases on iTunes.

- For providers that are supported, sign in to the cable provider for **single sign-on.**

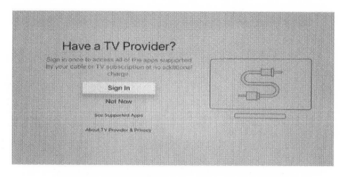

- Enable **Home Screen Syncing** if you want the apps and Home screen to always be up to date across your multiple Apple TVs.

- To activate location services, select **"Enable Location Services"** otherwise, click on **"Disable Location Services."**

- To automatically download Apple's Aerial screensavers, click on **Automatically Download** if not, choose **Not Now.**

- On the analytics screen, choose **"Send to Apple"** or **"Don't Send"** whichever you desire.

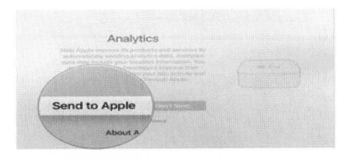

- Then select if you would like to share **App Analytics** with developers or not.

- Finally, accept the **Terms and Conditions.**

- And you are good to go!

How to Manually Set Up Your New Apple TV

If you would rather manually set up your device, follow the steps below

- Click the Siri remote trackpad to pair it with your TV.

- Choose your preferred **Language** from the list.
- Select your current **Country.**
- Select whether or not you want to use Siri.
- Then click on **Set Up Manually.**

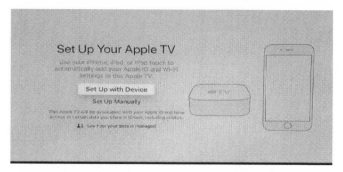

- Select your preferred Wi-Fi network and input the password.

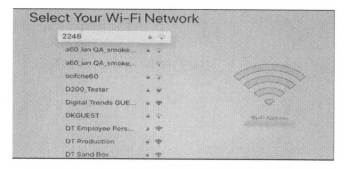

- Click on **Continue** for your TV to activate.
- On the next screen, click on **Apple ID** to input your existing ID or select "**Use**

Different Apple IDs for iTunes and iCloud" for those that have more than one Apple IDs. Then continue the steps below. If you have only one ID, skip these steps.

- If entering separate iTunes and iCloud credentials, input your **iCloud email address** on the next screen and then tap **Continue.**

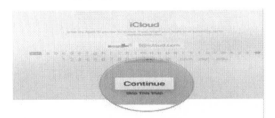

- Input your iCloud password on the next screen and tap **Continue.**
- Then input your iTunes email address if entering a separate iTunes and iCloud credentials and tap **Continue.**

- Input your iTunes password and tap **Continue.**

- Select when you would like the system to request for a **Password** after making purchases on iTunes.

- For providers that are supported, sign in to the cable provider for **single sign-on.**

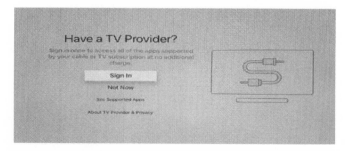

- Enable **Home Screen Syncing** if you want the apps and Home screen to always be up to date across your multiple Apple TVs.

- To activate location services, select **"Enable Location Services"** otherwise, click on **"Disable Location Services."**

- To automatically download Apple's Aerial screensavers, click on **Automatically Download,** if not, choose **Not Now.**

- On the analytics screen, choose **Send to Apple** or **Don't Send** whichever you desire.

- Then select if you would like to share **app analytics** with developers or not.

- Finally, accept the **Terms and Conditions.**

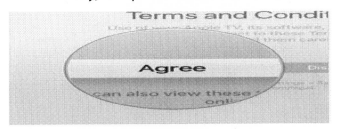

- And you are good to go!

How to Set up HDR and 4K

By default, the Apple TV 4K should automatically show contents available in 4K once you have a supported TV, contents and apps. However, you can still take some steps to improve your experience.

First confirm that your television supports the HDR and 4K. Then enable **Match Dynamic Range** feature on your Apple TV to give priority to HDR modes as well as refresh rates that best suits the movie or TV show you are watching instead of the highest standard matched by your TV. To do this, follow the steps below:

- Go to **Settings app** on your Apple TV.

- Click on **Video and Audio.**

- Then select **Match Content.**

- On the next screen, select **Match Frame Rate** and **Match Dynamic Range**

While **Match Dynamic Range** feature would show all contents that supports Dolby Vision, the **Match Frame Rate feature** uses the frame rate intended for the TV Show or movie. So, this means that movies will then be displayed in 24 frames per second instead of the experimental 60 or 30 frames per second.

The next thing would be to confirm that you are using a HDMI cable that supports 4K or HDR.

Apple advises that you go for one that has Dolby Vision certification which is what Apple used to test the TV 4K.

Finally, ensure to update the software of your TV.

How to Check for HDR and 4K on Apple TV

The simplest way to test for this is to swipe from the top of your screen downwards using your Apple TV remote. This would let you know if you are streaming in 4K. to confirm for HDR, return to the settings for **Match Content screen.** After selecting the option for **Match Dynamic Range,** the picture on your TV is expected to sputter a bit and then change. If this happens, it means you are set.

If you still require further proof, pair your Mac device together with the Apple TV. To do this, you need to download Apple's XCode developer tool as well as ensure that the Apple TV and Mac device is connected to the same Wi-Fi network. Then follow the steps below:

- Open XCode and select **Window**
- On the next screen, select **"Devices and Simulators."**
- Then go to the Apple TV 4K settings app, click on **"Remotes and Devices."**
- After which you select **"Remote App and Devices."**
- Go to the device manager for the XCode and select **"Apple TV."**
- A 6-digit pin would show on your Apple TV, input it on your Mac device.
- Then go to the settings app in the Apple TV and click on the **new Developer** menu.
- Then enable **Playback HUD.**

With this activated, whenever you are watching a movie, you would see a new developer HUD pop up on your screen showing you all the technical details about the movie or content. You would see whether its HDR, the resolution, the frame rate, the refresh rate and lots more.

How to Set up Dolby Atmos

Dolby Atmos support got to the Apple TV 4k when the tvOS 12 was launched. With the audio format, sound is projected towards you as well as around and above you to give that theater-like feeling in your sitting room. To get started, you need a speaker and a A/V receiver or sound bar that is Dolby Atmos enabled to use with your Apple TV.

Steps to Connect Dolby Atmos System to your Apple TV

If it is a Dolby Atmos hardware that you are using, you will plug your Apple TV 4k into the Dolby Atmos hardware then plug the hardware to your TV.

- Plug in the HDMI cable of your Apple TV 4k into the **HDMI In Port** of the Dolby Atmos A/V receiver or sound bar.

- Plug another HDMI cable into the HDMI Out or HDMI-ARC port of your A/V receiver or sound bar.

- Let the other end of the second HDMI cable go into the port in your TV.

- Ensure that the Dolby Atmos hardware and your Apple TV 4k are connected to power.

How to Confirm that Dolby Atmos is Enabled on your Apple TV

- Launch the **settings** app from the Apple TV.

- Click on **Video and Audio.**

- Click on **Audio Format**

- Then click on **immersive Audio** to confirm that **Dolby Atmos** is on.

- If Dolby Atmos is off, you would have to change how you set up your sound system.

How to Activate Siri on Apple TV

To activate Siri, simply hold down the Siri button located on your Siri remote. This is the button with the microphone icon on it, at the left part of your remote.

The Siri Remote/ Apple TV Remote

The Apple TV comes with the Siri remote which is a long and slim remote that has the Volume, Play/Pause, TV and Menu buttons as well as the Siri button. In some countries that are able to access Siri, you can use Siri to launch apps on your Apple TV as well as play moves, TV episodes and music. You can also check the weather, sport scores, play games and even check stocks.

The Siri remote is built to navigate through the interface, apps and keyboard of the Apple TV. With the Home button, you can go straight to the TV home screen or to the TV app. The glass trackpads located at the top of your remote gives you access to swipe through the interface of your TV and you can also click it just as you have on the Mac trackpad, to make your selections.

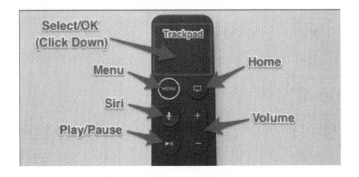

How to Use the TV Button

This button serves as a shortcut to the TV app.
But you can modify this to serve as the home
button.

- Double press the TV button to view the
  apps you used recently in Multitasking.
- To go directly to **Up Next** in the TV app
  from any part of the TV screen, press once
  on the TV button.
- Then click on the TV button again to
  return to the home screen.

How to Use the Menu button

- Press down the menu button to exit an app.
- While on the Apple TV home screen, press the menu button to go to the first app in the home tray.

- For 2 seconds, hold down the menu button to go to the home screen from any part of the TV screen.

- Select the first app you can see in the home tray and press the menu button to exit or start the screen saver.

How to Change the Home Button Function

- Go to settings on the Apple TV.

- Navigate to **Remotes and Devices.**

- Click on **Home button.**

- Select either the TV app or Home screen option by pressing the touch surface.

How to Use the Play/Pause Button

This button is used to control media contents on the Apple TV.

- To play or pause contents including games, movies and music, press the **Play/ Pause button.**

- When typing, click on the **Play/Pause button** to toggle between lower and upper case.

- Hold down the trackpad for a second to go into jiggly mode and then press the **Play/Pause button** to view the app options.

- While playing music in the music app and on the home screen, jump to the current song playing by pressing and holding the Play/Pause button.

How to Use the Volume Control Button

T

his button is used to turn down or up audio once the Siri remote is connected to the Apple TV.

- To reduce the volume of your TV, press the minus (-) button
- To increase the volume of your TV, press the plus (+) button

How to use the Siri button

This Button is your access to all the things that Siri can do.

- For tips on how to use Siri, press the Siri button.

- To activate Siri, press and hold the button.

- To talk to Siri, hold the Siri button and speak directly into the remote microphone. Release the button once you are done to get a response.

How to Use the Remote Trackpad

The trackpad is one of the features that distinguishes the Apple TV as it is only few traditional television remote controls that have the trackpad. The concept is concrete and makes a whole lot of sense once you understand the idea.

How to Identify the Location of the Trackpad
To know the side of the remote that is the trackpad, take a close look at the surface of the front of the remote. The bottom of the remote has a glossy finish while the top part has a matte finish. The remote trackpad is the matte finish part of the remote.

How to Swipe the Trackpad

When you swipe on the trackpad, you are able to scroll around the screen, brewing and fast forward music and movies as well as control movement in supported video games. The trackpad is quite Sensitive and is able to recognize slow and fast swipes. To use the trackpad,

- Place your thumb on the trackpad.
- Gently swipe your thumb down, up, right or left to scroll through your device.
- Begin from the far edge of the trackpad and swipe towards the other end to quickly scroll through stuffs.
- To scroll slowly through a few things, swipe your thumb slowly on the trackpad.
- When playing games, you can swipe the trackpad in a circular motion. If done when not playing games£/ would only make the icons to dance.

How to Tap the Trackpad on The Siri Remote

You can swipe the trackpad to scroll through several items

However, there are times you would want to just move on a spot. Lightly tap on the trackpad to scroll an item per time

- Place your thumb on the trackpad.
- Tap the trackpad lightly to the right, left, bottom or top to go one step per time. If you press down on the trackpad, it would select an item.
- Continue tapping until you get to your desired destination.

Note that pressing is different from tapping.

How to Select with the Trackpad

Press down on the trackpad to select, similar to clicking on a laptop's trackpad.

- Place your thumb on the trackpad.
- To select something, press down on the trackpad.

- Press the trackpad in two quick successions to double click in games and apps that support the feature.
- To put the desired app in jiggle mode when selecting an app, hold down the trackpad.

How to Adjust the Trackpad Sensitivity

If you feel the trackpad is too fast or too slow, you can adjust the sensitivity. You may need this mostly when playing games that require you use precise movement with the trackpad.

- Go to the settings app
- Click on **Remotes and Devices.**
- Then choose **Touch Surface Tracking.**

- Depending on what you need, select medium, slow or fast from the list.

What Can the Apple TV do

The Apple TV is one smart TV device that you can use to stream movies and TV shows by plugging it into any TV. The Apple TV is much more than just a streaming device as there are several things that you can do with the Apple TV other than watching Netflix. You can even use the Apple TV to replace the Spectrum cable box! You can use your Apple TV to watch NASA, turn it into a digital picture frame, achieve your weight loss goals with the workout apps or use as a display for your iPhone and laptops. From workouts to productivity to gaming, there is almost an endless list of things the Apple TV can do. Most of the times, the Apple TV allows you do more than you can achieve with the Smart TV coupled with the updates that Apple release every few months to take care of bugs and add better features.

The list below states some of the things that the Apple TV can do

1. Watch Live TV without using a cable
2. Play Party games
3. Rent TV shows and movies
4. Replace your cable box
5. Use Siri to start a show on the Apple TV.
6. Stream Cinemax, HBO, Showtime and others.
7. View your photos on your TV.
8. Mirror your iPhone or Mac on your TV.
9. Educate your kids.
10. Ask Siri to search for shows
11. Watch TV without disturbing anyone
12. Stream music

13. Control your home and lights
14. Get back to shape
15. Shop and find new styles
16. Find entertainment when lazy
17. Watch live sports on your Apple TV
18. Type your passwords with the iPhone as a remote
19. Listen to Dolby Atmos
20. Play games on the Apple TV
21. Control your sound system and your TV
22. Watch affordable 4K TV and movies

Inbuilt Apple TV Apps

Your Apple TV comes with the following apps by default

- **App store:** for accessing 3rd party TV apps.
- **iTunes TV Shows:** for TV shows shown on the iTunes store, includes the ones you rented or purchased previously.

48

- **iTunes Movies:** for movies shown on the iTunes store, includes the ones you rented or purchased previously
- **Music:** an app where your personal music is stored as well as access to the whole Apple music library which includes music videos.
- **Photos:** an app where you can access your current iCloud photo Library, Shared Photo streams and Photo streams.
- **Settings:** to modify or configure your TV settings.
- **Computers:** all the iTunes video libraries and music you added to home sharing would be seen here.
- **Search:** the universal search bar for the Apple TV.

Key features and Remote Tips

- When you ask Siri "what should I watch today?" it would display a menu of suggested shows and movies at the lower end of your screen with all the recommendations daily handpicked by editors to display what is buzzworthy.

- Click on the home button of your remote twice and it would show your recently used apps while allowing you to switch between apps without first going to the home screen.

- You can use the remote to move apps you use often to your home screen for quicker access.

- Easily organize apps into folders on the Apple TV.

- When you highlight a title in **Up Next,** tap and hold to give you a fast shortcut like marking episodes you have viewed previously.

- Click on the Play button on any title in the list for **Watch Now** to get the movie play instantly.

- Ask Siri to add any iTunes movies to your queue for **Up Next** movies.
- To resume binge watching, ask Siri to play "TV Show X".

How to Pair an Apple Remote with the Apple TV

The Apple TV is one of the most versatile media streaming boxes available in the market. However, one challenge you may encounter with the Apple TV has to do with the remote. At times, the Apple remote may disconnect in error or get damaged and you would need to buy another one. Which means you would need to pair the new remote to your Apple TV. Follow the steps below to pair your remote with the Apple TV.

The Apple TV remote/ the Siri remote is designed to pair automatically with the Apple TV 4k without any action from your end. So, if you notice that your Apple TV is not responding to your Apple TV remote, the first thing you should do is to recharge the remote. There is no physical battery indicator on the remote and you may not also have seen the warning on the TV screen that the battery is low. Use a lighting cable to plug in the remote for a minimum of 30 minutes and see if it would bring the remote back to life.

If the challenge is with the volume buttons not responding, ensure that there are no objects blocking the infrared receiver on the Sound bar, TV or A/V receiver. The Apple TV remote controls the volume of the devices by using line-of-sight infrared.

If you try all these and the remote still is not working, then follow the steps below to manually re-pair the Apple remote:

- Ensure that the Apple TV is powered up. A white LED light should show on the front of the Apple TV. If you are not seeing the white LED, unplug the Apple TV, allow

about 6 seconds before you plug it back
in. The white LED should come up now.

- Turn on your TV and confirm that the input
  is set to the right HDMI port, also check
  that the Apple TV home screen is visible.

- Hold the Apple TV remote with the face up
  and few inches from the Apple TV box.

- Press the remote's **Menu and Volume Up**
  buttons at same time and hold for
  approximately five seconds. Let your eyes
  be on your TV screen. If you receive a
  message to place your remote closer to

the Apple TV, then place the remote on the Apple TV box itself.

- Once paired, a message would popup on the screen alerting you that the Apple TV remote has been paired successfully.
- If you did not get this message and the Apple TV isn't still responding to the remote buttons, unplug the Apple TV again, allow 6 seconds before you plug it back and carry out steps 2 to 4 again.

If peradventure the Apple TV remote is still not working after trying al these steps, it then means that the remote is defective and you would have to call Apple support or walk into your preferred Apple store for assistance.

How to charge the Siri Remote

As is common with other remote control, the Siri Remote battery would eventually run down, although it may take a long time but it would happen. However, rather than having to change the battery of the remote, Apple made it easy as you can charge your Siri Remote with the lighting cable. Simply plug your remote into your lighting cable and enjoy your movies while the remote charges up.

How to Activate the Apple TV Screensaver

The Apple TV screensavers are beautiful and with each release of the tvOS, we see new and better improvements. Follow the steps below to activate your TV screensaver.

- Go to the TV home screen then click the **Menu button** of your Siri remote quickly for 3 times to activate the screensaver.

Rent Movies & TV Shows

The Apple TV is the center of your home entertainment system. You can stream movies and TV shows from a wide range of services.

This includes watching new releases from iTunes or watching your favorite TV shows on Hulu Plus. You can use Netflix and other streaming services so that you are covered when it comes to watching old, new, odd and super popular movies.

You'll also find PBS, CBS News, Vimeo, YouTube, VEVO, The Weather Channel, Facebook Videos and several apps that you can use to stream movies and videos with a subscription or a purchase.

Ask Siri What to Watch

If you are uncertain of what you should watch, simply say to Siri, "What should I watch?" and Siri would display popular and new selections. You can also ask Siri for "What shows are trending currently?" or "Show me popular movies."

How to Jump to Live TV

If you have apps that provide live streaming of recent broadcasts, you can go straight to the live feed without navigating through the menu options. Hold the Siri button and say "Watch ESPN" or "Watch CBS"

Find Free Streaming Options

When in search of what to watch, do not search inside the apps, use the Apple TV's universal voice search to search through all the installed apps and informs you of the available options. The amazing thing about this voice search is that it could find a free way of watching a movie or TV show that you aren't aware of.

To find these contents, press down the Siri button on the remote and say to Siri, "Show me [the name of the thing you're looking for]." Pick your preferred item from the list displayed at the end of your screen. On the search result screen, look for the line that says **Available On,** underneath the description for your options. Click on **Open In** to access the video from your preferred app.

Do Not Miss Hard to Hear Dialogue

You no longer have to miss out mumbled words with the Apple TV. If you did not get what a character said in the movie or show, simply hold down the Siri button and say to Siri, "what did he/she say?" once you release the button, the video would rewind to some seconds and also turn on the closed captioning for some seconds while boosting the volume of your audio.

How to Change What You Can Do with the Home Button

You can choose what you would like to see when you press the Home button on your Siri remote. You can use it as a shortcut to the TV app or use it to access the Home screen. To carry out this change, follow the steps below:

- Go to **Settings** on your Apple TV.
- Click on **Remotes and Devices**
- Choose **Home button** and then click on the touch surface of your remote to choose either **TV app** or **Home screen.**

How to Switch between Apps

Similar to the App switcher available on iOS, you can easily switch between apps on the Apple TV. You can also force close an app. Follow the steps below.

- Double press the **Home button** on your Siri remote to activate the Apple TV App switcher.
- Swift left and right with the remote's trackpad to move between apps.
- Click on the trackpad to choose an app you want to open.

- If you would like to exit Multitasking without clicking on any app, simply press the menu button.

How to Close Apps

To close an app, follow the steps below:

- Double press the **Home button** on your Siri remote to activate the Apple TV App switcher.
- This would display all the open apps. Swipe up on your desired app to close it.

How to Skip Backward and Forward

While viewing a movie on your TV, you can move back or forward by clicking on the left or right edge respectively of the Siri Remote trackpad. This action would move the video forward or backward by 10 seconds.

Also, you do not need to bring up the timeline of a video to drag the play bar when you want to rewind or fast forward. Simply press the right part of the trackpad and hold to fast forward. Press the left part of the trackpad and hold to rewind.

How to Scrub through Videos

You also have the option of scrubbing through videos if you do not want to rewind/fast forward or skip. The solution is simple if you know the exact place in the video you want to begin from.

- Pause the video by pressing the **Play/Pause** button then swipe right and left on your trackpad to scrub backward and forward through the video.

How to Enable Subtitle on a Playing Video

In case you started playing a video before remembering to turn on the subtitles, you no longer need to exit the video to enable the subtitles. Rather, while the video is playing, swipe down on the trackpad. You would see a summary of the movie or the show you are watching on your screen and the option to adjust audio settings and enable subtitles.

How to Reboot your Apple TV

Whenever you need to reboot your TV, you can perform this without going to the settings app. Simply hold down the Menu and Home buttons simultaneously on your Siri Remote until you see the Apple TV light begin to blink. This would force the TV to start rebooting.

How to Create App Folders

Do you know that you can uncluttered your Apple TV home screen by grouping the Apps into folders? How to do this:

- Go to the Home screen.
- Use the trackpad to press and hold on an app icon until it begins to jiggle.
- Then press the button for **Play/Pause.**
- With your trackpad, select the option to **create a new folder.**

- Input your preferred folder name.
- Then drag apps into the respective folders.

How to Move Apps into Folders

An easy way to quickly move apps into different folders is to press the app icon for some seconds to get it to jiggle and then click the **Play/Pause** button and choose select **Move to [folder name]** to move the apps quickly into any desired folder or to send it back to the Home screen.

How to Rearrange Apps

You can arrange how apps are placed in your Apple TV. To do so

- Go to an app you want to move, press and hold the trackpad on that app
- Swipe the trackpad to move the app down, up, right or left.

- Click on the trackpad to drop the app in its new place on the home screen.

How to Quickly Switch Between Upper and Lower Characters

Using the Apple TV on screen keyboard can be quite stressful, particularly if you have to use a combination of uppercase and lowercase characters. Although you can use your iPhone's Apple TV app to do this, however, I have a better way for you to use your Siri remote to add text.

- To switch between lower- and upper-case characters while typing text, simply press the **Play/ Pause** button on your remote.

What Siri Can and Cannot Do (Siri Commands)

One of the best features of the Apple TV is the integration of Siri. The Apple virtual assistant has a long list of what it can do including searching for contents across several media providers, information on specified sports celebrities, movies, weather and lots more.

When you ask the virtual assistant, Siri, what it can search for, you would hear it say "I can search by ratings (like TV-G or PG), people (director, actor, character name, producer, guest star, or writer), title, age (like teen or kid-friendly), reviews (like worst or best), dates (like 2019 or the 90s), studio, episodes and seasons. And of course, I can search by genre."

What Siri Can do/ List of Siri Commands

1.   Siri can search for TV Shows and Movies

Siri is designed with a search feature that is robust and has multi-layer filtering. In case you need information or details on any movie you had previously seen but cannot remember the details?

You can ask Siri as it definitely would know the details.

When you say to Siri "What should I watch tonight?", it would display on your screen list of popular television shows and movies in iTunes as well as other apps for media streaming like Hulu, Netflix, Showtime, HBO and others.

- Say to Siri, "What are some current [genre] TV shows/ movies?" And Siri would reply back with a list of all the current titles within the genre you requested.

- You can limit the search result by saying "Only the best ones" or "Only the new ones" and the search results would automatically filter using your requested topic. You can add several criteria to your search. For instance, you can say to Siri, "Show me popular romance movies from the 90s" and also include "Only the best ones."

- Another question to ask Siri is, "What [genre] movies did [producer/ director/ actor/] do from [decade]?"

- If you have a hard time trying to remember the name of the movie where your two favorite actors starred in, simply ask Siri, "What movie stars [actor] and [actor]?"

- You can conclude the question with asking Siri "Who else starred in the movie?"

- Do you need to remember the actor that played a particular role in a TV show or movie, Siri can help out when you ask, "Who played [the character] in [TV show /movie]?"

The more you interact with Siri, the smarter it gets. You can request for multiple criteria in one question. You could say, "Search YouTube for kitten fails" or "I need action films from the 1970s."

2. **Siri Helps to Playback Actions**

Imagine watching a TV show or movie with a buddy and you need a little help. Siri is like having a close friend sit beside you, the only difference is that Siri would accommodate all your questions.

- If you need to quickly find a TV show or movie, all you need is to tell Siri to "Play [name]."

- You may have started a movie about 6 months ago which you did not remember to finish up. Apple TV would automatically resume from the last scene you viewed.

You can ask Siri to "Play from the beginning."

- Also, Siri would automatically pause or play a content on your request.

- If you did not understand the marble-mouthed mumbles of an author in a TV show or movie, simply ask Siri, "What did he say?" And the movie would rewind for approximately 15 seconds which would also automatically turn on the closed captioning for about 30 seconds.

- Say you left the room for some minutes while watching a movie and you need to see what happened in a particular scene. Just tell Siri to "Rewind [number of] minutes." You can also instruct Siri to skip forward to a certain time.

- Curious to know the celebrities in a movie you are viewing currently, Say to Siri, "Who stars in this?" and a list containing the actors would display at the end of your TV screen.

- When available, you can ask Siri to "Turn on closed captions"

- Viewing a foreign movie? Ask Siri to "Turn on subtitles."

3. **Siri Can Help with Music**

You can surf through the Music app on the Apple TV for music using the song title, album or artist. You can also make Siri your own personalized deejay.

- As said earlier, you can ask Siri to pause or play content just by saying the word and like we have for videos, you can fast forward or rewind to a certain time in a song

- You can ask Siri to "Play [song/ album]." You would get the best result if you include the artist's name too.
- When you tell Siri "Play My Music," it would begin to play songs from your iCloud music library. (Note: you can only use the My Music app on your Apple TV when you are signed into iCloud)
- If you want Siri to play a title you have in your music library, say "Play [songs] by [artist] in My Music"
- To remove a song from rotation, you can say, "Never play this song again"
- To add a music to your Like list, you should say, "I like this song,"
- To move on to the next music, say to Siri, "Skip this song"
- To know more details about an audio you are listening to, say to Siri, "What album is

this on?" Or "What is the name of this song?"

- To know the name of an artist for a playing music, say to Siri, "Who sang this song?". Then if you want to see more songs by the same artist, say to Siri, "Show me albums by this artist"

4. **Siri can Help Search for Games and Apps**

You can ask Siri to display a particular app from the Apple TV App store and you would see a list of query results in the Siri tray, which should include what you are searching for. To go straight to the download view for a particular app, say to Siri, "Download [app name]"

5. **Siri can Help to turn off the Light**

As long as you are signed into iCloud on your Apple TV, Siri can control your HomeKit devices that are connected. Ask Siri to "Lock the front door" or "Turn off the bedroom light" and it would oblige you so long as the HomeKit is connected.

6. **Siri Knows Weather and Time in all parts of the world**

You can ask Siri to update you on weather predictions in any parts of the world.

- For the current weather forecast, say to Siri, "How hot/cold will it get today?"

- To know the current conditions for today, say to Siri, "What is the temperature?"

- When going on a trip and you need to know what the travel conditions would be like, say to Siri "Will it rain on [date] in [location]?"

- To know if you should head out with an umbrella when leaving home, ask Siri, "Will its rain/snow?"

- To know the week's weather forecast, ask Siri, "What will the weather be like this week?"

- You can also ask Siri when the sun would go down in Canada.

- To know the time in a particular location, simply ask Siri, "What time is it in [location]?"

7. Siri knows Sports

You can always ask Siri an update on the games you missed, detailed info on a particular player or the next time your team would play.

- To know the current score on a game, say to Siri, "What is the score of [game]?"

- To know your team's most recent score, say to Siri, "Did [team] win the game?"

- To see the predicted odds for a point spreads or to see the point spread itself, say to Siri, "What was the point spread of [game]"

- To know when next your team is scheduled to play again, say to Siri, "When does [team] play next?"

- You can also ask Siri to know which team have the best performance this season by asking "Who is going to win?"

- To know who plays a particular position in a team, ask Siri.

- To know a player's stat, ask Siri, "How many [actions] did [player] have in the last game"

8. Siri Also Follows Stock Market

You can ask Siri to fill you in on some basic information for the stock market of S&P 500, DOW and NASDAQ.

- You can ask Siri "how is a particular stock doing"

- To get information on the 3 major stock markets, say to Siri, "How are the markets doing?"

- For the day's opening and closing numbers, say to Siri, "What was the open/close of the markets?"

9. Other Things Siri can do on Apple TV

- Ask Siri to flip a coin, roll the dice or use the in-built Magic 8-ball to get random answers and numbers.

- Ask Siri to "Open iTunes" and you would get the option to choose from Movies, TV shows, Trailers, or Music.

- When within view of toolbar for any app like subscription, search, home and the likes, just say the name of the tool for Siri to automatically take you to the new page.

- To launch any app installed on the Apple TV, say to Siri, "Launch [app name]."

- To go straight to the home screen from any app, say to Siri, "Go back to the Home screen,"

What Siri Cannot Do

While we have a vast list of things that Siri can do on the Apple TV, there are still some things that virtual assistant cannot do.

- Siri cannot search the web.

- Siri cannot add music or create playlists in the music app.
- Siri can't close apps opened in the multitasking screen.
- Siri can't search contents stored in your hard drive.
- Siri cannot search libraries under home sharing.

How to Check Battery Level of the Siri Remote

You do not need to wait until the TV alerts you before you know the battery level of your remote. Follow the steps below to check the battery level.

- Switch on the Apple TV.
- Launch the settings app.
- Choose **Remotes and Devices.**
- Then select **Remote.**

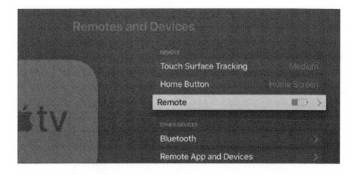

- In this section, you would see serial number for your device, battery percentage and firmware version.

How to Charge the Siri Remote from a Wall Socket

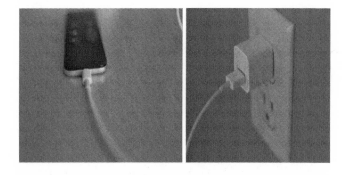

To charge your Siri remote from a wall outlet, follow the steps below

- Plug the USB part of the lighting cable into a wall plug adapter similar to what comes with the iPad or iPhone.

- Let the 8-pin part of the lighting cable go into the Lighting port of the Siri remote, located at the bottom side of the remote.

- Now, insert the USB wall plug adapter into the wall socket.

- Let it remain plugged in until the remote is done charging.

- Once charging is done, disconnect the lighting cable from the Siri remote.

- Follow the steps above to see the battery level to know when the remote is done charging as there is no light indicator.

How to Charge the Remote Using your Computer

You can charge the remote with your computer instead of a wall outlet. Follow the steps below to do so

- Let the 8-pin part of the lighting cable go into the Lighting port of the Siri remote, located at the bottom side of the remote.
- Plug the USB part of the lighting cable into the port for USB on your laptop computer or desktop.
- Let it remain plugged in until the remote is done charging.

- Once charging is done, disconnect the lighting cable from the Siri remote.
- Follow the steps above to see the battery level to know when the remote is done charging as there is no light indicator.

The battery of the Siri Remote takes a long time before it gets drained usually up to 6 months. So, you would not need to charge it often if you do not use the Apple TV daily, while you would charge it more if you play lots of video games.

How to Use the Siri Remote to Play Video
Once you know the video clip, TV show or movie you want to view, hit the Play/ pause button.

- Launch the app you want to select the video form (e.g. Hulu)
- Choose the video you wish to play.

- Click on the Play/Pause button on your remote or press down on the remote's trackpad.
- Press down and hold the right side of the trackpad to fast forward contents while you use the left side to rewind.
- Click on the trackpad from the new spot to play your content.

How to Access Additional Options while Watching a Video

While watching a video, you can access some additional options like enabling subtitles, getting movie info and adjusting options for audio.

- Launch the app you want to select the video form (e.g. Hulu)
- Choose the video you wish to play.
- Click on the Play/Pause button on your remote or press down on the remote's trackpad.

- Swipe down on your remote trackpad to pull up the additional options. You would see the info screen displayed.
- Swipe to your right to view audio options and to your right to activate subtitles.
- To hide the option menu, swipe up on the trackpad.
- If the progress bar does not automatically disappear, gently tap the trackpad to hide it.

How to Play Audio Content

- Launch the app you want to select the audio from (e.g. iTunes)
- Choose the audio you wish to play.
- Click on the Play/Pause button on your remote or press down on the remote's trackpad.
- Press down and hold the right side of the trackpad to fast forward contents. Hold the left side of the trackpad to rewind.

- To skip a selection, click the right side of the remote trackpad or click the left side of the remote trackpad to return to the start of a song.
- To replay the last played track, double click on the left side of the trackpad

How to Access Additional Options While Playing Audio

- Launch the app you want to select the audio from.
- Choose the audio you wish to play.
- Click on the Play/Pause button on your remote or press down on the remote's trackpad.
- To view the list of audio tracks, press the trackpad.
- To call up the **More** option, swipe up on the remote trackpad. The icon looks more like an ellipsis (...)

How to put an app into jiggly mode

You need to first know how to get an app to jiggle before you can delete or move an app. When you are able to get the app to jiggle, then you can perform any action.

- Click on the app you want to jiggle.
- Press down and hold the remote trackpad Until the app hovers and starts to jiggle.
- Once it begins to jiggle you can delete or move.

How to Move an App with the Siri Remote

If you would like all your apps to follow a specific order to give you a clean interface, follow the steps below on how to move the apps

- Click on the app you wish to move.
- Follow the steps above to get it into the jiggle mode.

- Then swipe down, up, right or left with your remote trackpad to get it to its new position.
- Click on the remote's trackpad to exit the jiggly mode.

How to Delete an App with the Siri Remote

You can download an app that you do not need and install it later in the future.

- Click on the app you wish to move.
- Follow the steps above to get it into the jiggle mode.
- Use your remote to press the Play/Pause button.
- Click on **Delete** when prompted and press down on the remote trackpad to delete the app.
- Repeat the action to delete all unwanted apps.

A faster way to easily delete several applications faster is shown below:

- Go to the settings app.
- Click on **General.**

- Then click on **Manage Storage.**
- Then click the trash can icon at the right of all the apps you want to delete.

How to Clear the Multitasking Tray

Most times you may not need to clear the Multitasking tray, however if your Apple TV begins to have issues or starts running slow, one solution would be to force close all apps. Follow the steps below

- Go to the home screen and then double click the **Home button** of the remote.
- First force-close the first app on the tray by swiping up on the trackpad.
- Repeat step 2 u till the Multitasking tray is empty.
- Press the menu button to exit Multitasking.

How to Control your TV with the Siri Remote

Apart from the Apart TV, you can also use the Siri remote to control other television. For instance, you can use the Siri remote to power on a television that supports HDMI-CEC. Follow the steps below to activate this function

- Go to **settings** on your Apple TV.
- Choose **Remotes and Devices**.
- Then select **Control TVs and Receivers** to read **On** if not previously enabled.

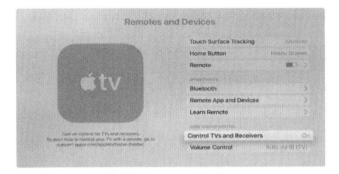

- Click on **Volume Control.**

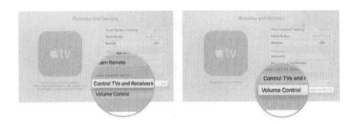

- Select from any of the available options:

Auto, TV via IR, Soundbar via IR or **Off.**

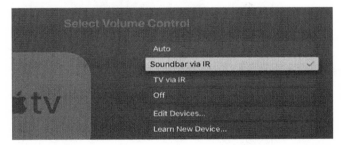

- If the options are not available, click on **Learn New Device** to link your TV with the Siri remote.

How to Restart your Apple TV with the Siri Remote

When your TV begins to misbehave, you can restart it just like to would restart an iPad or iPhone. While you would find the restart section under the settings app in your television, however, you can use your Siri remote to quickly restart the TV. You restart your device to fix minor glitches like frozen screen.

- Press down the menu button and hold it.

- Also hold down the TV button of your remote at the same time

- Continue to hold both buttons until you sew the status light of your Apple TV start to flash.
- Release the two buttons.
- The screen would go black for a few seconds then the Apple logo would appear.

How to Use the Remote to Put the TV to Sleep/ Wake

You can either wait for the device to sleep on its own or you can manually use the remote to put it in the sleep mode. Follow the steps below:

- Press the TV/Home button and hold it for a second.
- From the popup, choose **Sleep**

- Your TV would go into sleep mode immediately.
- Press any button on your remote to wake the device.

How to Set When the TV Goes to Sleep

Putting your device to sleep when not in use can hemp to conserve battery and show off your beautiful screensaver. You can set the Apple TV to sleep at a specified time or period of the day.

- Launch the settings app.
- Click on **General**

- Under General, click on **Sleep After.**

- On the next screen, you can set when you want Apple to go to sleep after defined time of inactivity. Options include **Never, 15 minutes, 30 minutes, one hour, five hours, or 10 hours.**

How to Manually Put your Apple TV to sleep

To manually shut down the Apple TV, follow the steps below:

- Launch the settings app.
- Then choose **sleep now.**

How to add a Game Controller to your TV

While it's okay to play games on your device using the Siri remote, it is an entirely awesome experience to use a dedicated game controller.

Products used for this review

- Steel series Nimbies
- Dual shock 4 Wireless Controller

How to pair a game controller to your Apple TV

- Switch on the controller. To turn on the SteelSeries Nimbus, switch the hold button to **ON**.

- If you have previously paired the controller, you may have to hold down the **Bluetooth** button.
- Launch the settings app on your Apple TV.
- Click on **remote and Devices.**

- Select **Bluetooth.**
- Look for your controller in the list of Bluetooth devices then click on your controller to pair it.
- Once paired successfully, you would now be able to play games with the paired controller.

How to pair a Game Controller to your Apple TV on tvOS 13

- Switch on the controller.
- Launch the settings app on your Apple TV.
- Click on **remote and Devices.**

- Select **Bluetooth.**
- Then click on **Pair Game Controller.**
- Follow the instructions on your TV screen to pair your Xbox wireless, DualShock or MFI controller.
- Find your controller in the Bluetooth devices link and click on it to pair.

- Now you can begin to play both your previously played games as well as new arcade games from Apple

How to Set Up A Universal Remote to Control Your Apple TV

Although most universal remotes should work with your Apple TV, it is important for you to read the instructions in the remote to ensure that it is compatible with the Apple TV. Once confirmed, follow the steps below to set it up for controlling your Apple TV.

- From the home screen, launch the settings app of your apple TV.
- From the menu, select **Remote and Devices.**

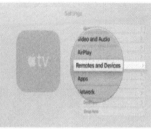

- Then choose **Learn Remote**
- Ensure that the universal remote is on. You have to also use an unused device setting.
- Click on **Start** to begin using the universal remote.

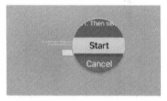

- On your universal remote, hold down the button you would like to use fir the **Up** function. Hold until the progress bar fills up.

- Do same action to select the button for the **Down** function on your universal remote.

- Do same action to select the button for the **Right and Left** function on your universal remote

- Do same action to select the button for the **Menu and Select** functions on your universal remote.

- Once done, type in a name for the remote and click on **Done.**

- On the next screen, click on "**Set up Playback button.**"

- On your universal remote, press and hold the button you would like to use for the

Play function. Hold until the progress bar fills up.

- On your universal remote, press and hold the button you would like to use fir the **Pause** function. Hold until the progress bar fills up

- On your universal remote, press and hold the button you would like to use fir the **Stop** function. Hold until the progress bar fills up

- On your universal remote, press and hold the button you would like to use fir the **Rewind** function. Hold until the progress bar fills up

- On your universal remote, press and hold the button you would like to use fir the

Fast-forward function. Hold until the progress bar fills up.

- On your universal remote, press and hold the button you would like to use fir the **Previous Track** function. Hold until the progress bar fills up

- On your universal remote, press and hold the button you would like to use fir the **Next Track** function. Hold until the progress bar fills up

- On your universal remote, press and hold the button you would like to use fir the **Skip Backward** function. Hold until the progress bar fills up.

- On your universal remote, press and hold the button you would like to use fir the **Skip Forward** function. Hold until the progress bar fills up

- Once done, click on **OK.**

The steps above would not only link your u universal remote to your Apple TV, it would also allow you to set the commands to buttons of your choice. Good news is that you can always remap the remote whenever you wish if you do not like how the buttons are placed.

How to Control Your HDTV with Apple TV Remote

With the Apple TV, you no longer need several remotes to control different medias and TV. Once the setting is right, the Siri remote can turn on your receiver, TV and Apple TV at same time while controlling the volume of the TV. To do this,

- Go to the settings app.
- Click on **General.**

 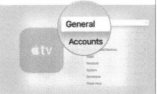

- Then select **Remotes and Devices.**

- First enable the **Control TVs and Receivers** menu by moving the switch to the right.

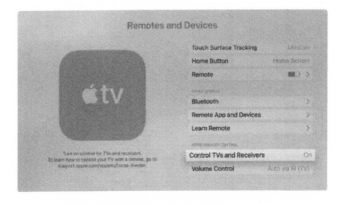

- Then click on **Volume Control** and select your preferred option. (select **Auto** if you are not sure of what to select)

How to Display Your iPad, iPhone or Mac on your Apple TV

You can use the Apple TV to project your iPad, iPhone or Mac to your HDTV. This is an awesome addition for playing videos from your device, viewing photos on a larger screen or giving a presentation. You would need to use Airplay Mirroring to achieve this. Airplay Mirroring is a feature built into the macOS, iOS, and tvOS. Ensure that the Apple TV and device you wish to project on the TV are both connected to same Wi-Fi network

How to Use Dark Mode at Night

The interface of the Apple TV is full of bright, big and appealing images and colors which may not be best to use when watching at Night or in the dark. For this, you may need to use a more muted look. You can enable the Apple TV's Dark Mode to make the home screen darker. Follow the steps below to enable Apple TV Dark Mode

- Go to the settings app.
- Click on **Appearance**
- Then click on **Dark** or **Automatic** if you want your system to be adjusted based on the time of the day.

How to Use Apple TV to Control Your Smart Home

If you make use of internet connected smart home devices like lights, thermostats and cameras in your home, you would need a smart home hub. The hub is useful as it helps the devices to communicate with each other while giving you total control over them using the internet. For Smart home devices that makes use of the Apple's HomeKit standard, you would not need to get a separate smart home hub as the Apple TV can play this role. Follow the steps below to enable this feature

- Go to the settings app on your home screen.
- Click on **Accounts**
- Then click on **iCloud.**
- Enable the option for **My Home** by toggling the switch to a connected status.

How to Confirm that Your Smart Home is Connected

If you have smart home devices that is HomeKit compatible, your iPad or Apple TV can serve as a hub to control them remotely using Siri on another iOS device. However, with a recent update to the tvOS, you can now directly control the HomeKit with the Siri Remote for Apple TV. If you are using the same iCloud account on both your iPhone and your Apple TV, the Apple Tv would automatically set itself up as a HomeKit Hub. To confirm that the setup is done correctly, follow the steps below:

- Go to the **Settings app.**
- Click on **Accounts**
- Then click on **iCloud.**
- Here, you should find a menu called **HomeKit.**
- Look out for your home name and confirm that it is showing as **Connected.**
- Once connected, you can use your voice to control your smart home devices with the Siri remote.

- You can also remotely control the smart home devices when away from home by using Siri on the Apple TV and a connected iPad or iPhone.

How to Pair Bluetooth Headphones and Keyboard

You can use all types of Bluetooth accessories with your Apple TV from wireless headphones to game controllers to keyboards and lots more. Simply connect the Bluetooth accessory to your Apple TV. Follow the steps below to perform the pairing.

- Launch the settings app on your Apple TV.
- Click on **Remote and Devices.**

- Select **Bluetooth.**
- Then click on the accessory you want to pair.
- For devices that requires a pin, you would be prompted to input the PIN.

How to Use the iPad, iPhone or Apple Watch as Your Remote Control

If you lose your Siri Remote or do not just fancy using the remote, you can use the iPad, iPhone or even Apple Watch to serve as your remote. For the Apple Watch and iPad, you would need to install the free **Remote app.** If using the Watch, you also need to install the remote on the iPhone that the watch is paired to. If your iPhone device is running iOS 11 and above, the controls are in-built into the control center.

How to Turn Apple TV into a Business Tool with Conference Room Display

Thanks to the Airplay, you can now project your computer or device on your TV. When Apple TV is in Conference Room Display mode, the TV becomes available for everyone to connect and use. Under this mode, the TV would show a screensaver as well as instructions on how to connect. Follow the steps below to enable the conference room display.

- Launch the settings app on your Apple TV.
- Click on **Airplay**
- Select **Conference Room Display**
- Then enable the **Conference Room Display** mode by toggling the switch to the right.

How to Enable One Home Screen

If you have more than one Apple TV, you would likely want all of them to have same options and apps but would you rather download and manually arrange the apps? You won't have to do this if you have the One Home Screen enabled. With this feature enabled, all your Apple TVs that have the same iCloud account would automatically sync in all the apps they have installed, including the apps arrangements, folders and lots more. Follow the steps below to enable this feature.

- Go to settings app.
- Click on **Accounts**
- Then select **iCloud**
- In the next screen, move the switch beside **One Home Screen** to the right to enable.

How to Customize Screensaver

While the Apple TV's aerial screensavers are beautiful and bring life to your living room in the form of high-resolution video, however, you can change the screensavers if you want something else as well as change the speed at which they update. Follow the steps below to do this

- Go to the settings app.
- Click on **General.**
- Then select **Screensaver.**
- Click on **Type** under which you would see the following options: Aerial, **Home Sharing, Apple Photos**, Music **Library** or **My Photos**. This last option would only show if you have opened the Photos app in the Apple TV and enabled the iCloud Photo Sharing.

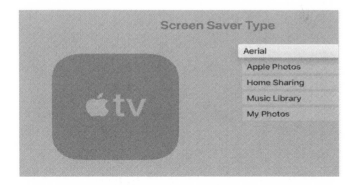

- Each of the selection has its own settings like transition between photos or how often should the system download new Aerial screensavers.

How to Automatically Install Apps

Just as you have it when you install an app in your iPad and it automatically gets installed on your iPhone, you can have same on the Apple TV so long as the app can work on the Apple TV. Follow the steps below to enable this feature.

- Launch the settings app.
- Click on **Apps.**
- Then click on **Automatically Install Apps** to enable the feature.

How to Use Your iPad or iPhone as a Keyboard

It can be difficult typing with the Apple TV remote. Luckily, with the iPad or iPhone, you can type in your search queries. When you click on a field to input text, it would trigger a notification on nearby linked iOS devices. This feature is called the Apple TV keyboard and can work with Apple TVs and iOS devices signed in with same Apple IDs so long as you have enabled Wi-Fi and Bluetooth. To use this feature,

- Click on the notification on any of the iOS devices.
- Then start typing with the keyboard on the screen.
- Whatever you type on your iOS device would show on the Apple TV screen.

How to Configure Loud Sounds

Another way you can use sounds at night without the need to wear headphones is to enable the **Reduce Loud Sounds** option. This option softens music and soft effect so that you can watch your movies or listen to your audio without disturbing the next person. To enable this feature, follow the steps below:

- Go to **Settings.**
- Click on **Video and Audio.**
- Then enable the **Reduce Loud Sounds** option

How to Stream any Audio to your Entertainment System

While the Apple Tv do not officially support apps like Google Play Music or Spotify, you can still use the Apple TV and Airplay to stream your favorite apps through your entertainment system. To do this, launch your music streaming or podcast of choice, play your audio, then look for Cast or Airplay icon within the app. If you are unable to locate the icon, swipe up from the end of the iPhone screen and activate Airplay from the Control Center. Choose your Apple TV and stream your music through your TV.

How to Follow Your Favorite Shows

The TV app serves as a TV guide for all your favorite streaming apps on the Apple TV. Once you login to your TV provider, all the compatible streaming apps that supports the single sign on feature would automatically sign you in. then the TV app would automatically start to track all the shows that you view in **Watch Now** under the **Up Next** section. As new episodes of those shows are released, you would see it at the front of the queue.

How to Enable Family Sharing

If family sharing is enabled on your iCloud account and you use the iCloud account to login to your Apple TV, all the contents purchased on that iCloud account would be shared in a single Apple TV. You would view all your previous purchases under the Purchased tab in the App Store, TV Shows apps and iTunes Movies.

To see the purchased contents of another user, go to the Purchased tab, click on **Family Sharing** then tap a User's photo.

To access music from another user's account,

- Go to settings.
- Click on **Accounts**
- Select **iTunes and App Store.**
- Then switch from your account to the desired user's account.

How to Capture the Apple TV Screen

If a content is not playing on the Apple TV, you can use the QuickTime on a Mac and a USB-C cable to record the Apple TV screen. To do this,

- Plug the USB-C cable into your Apple TV, at the back

- Plug the other end of the cable into the Mac port.

- Launch QuickTime.

- Go to **File** and click on **New Movie Recording.**

- A window would appear on the screen, click the arrow facing downward beside the record button.

- Then choose your Apple TV from the dropdown menu list.

- You would get a live preview of the screen of your Apple TV on your Mac.

- Click the record button to begin capturing the screen.

How to Add Apple TV Remote to Your iOS Control Center

The Siri Remote can control the Apple TV but the iOS also have the Apple TV remote app. However, if you would not want to have to launch an app each time you need to use the TV remote app, there is another way to go through it. With the control center, you would have access to all the remote features that you need. Simply swipe down on your iOS device and click on the Apple TV icon that you would find in the control center. You can navigate, play and pause, head to home screen and even use Siri. The only thing you may be unable to do with the Control Center's TV remote is to adjust the volume. The Control Center's TV remote is programmed to automatically install itself after you must have downloaded the Apple TV remote app. You can follow the steps below to manually activate it, if it is not activated.

- Go to the settings app
- Click on **Control Center.**
- Then select **Customize Controls** to open it.
- Scroll to the bottom and click on the green + sign next to Apple TV Remote.

Troubleshooting Tips for the Apple TV

How to Force Close an App

Should you experience any trouble with using an app, you can forcefully exit the app, to do this, just hold down the menu button located on the Siri remote. As simple as that. Follow the steps below to force close an app.

- Switch on the Apple TV.
- Go to the home screen
- On the Siri remote, double click the Apple TV home button. This is the button on the remote that has a TV icon on it.
- Swipe the trackpad to the right to look for the apps you want to force close
- To force close the app, swipe up on the trackpad.
- Press the menu button on your remote to exit multitasking. The menu button has the word **menu** on it.

How to Reset a TV Glitch

If you are experiencing issues with the tvOS and the apps, you may need to perform a hard reset. Follow the steps below to perform a hard reset.

- Go to the Settings app.
- Click on **System**
- Then click on **Reset.**
- Select **Reset** to erase all settings and content and restore your TV to factory settings or select **Reset and Update** to not only restore to factory settings but also to update your TV to the most current tvOS version.

Note that when you do this, it would delete all the local contents that are not backed up to iCloud including saved games.

How to Force Restart your Apple TV

If experiencing issues with the Apple TV and
apps, you can force restart the TV by following
the steps below:

- On your Siri remote, hold down the menu
  button.
- While holding the menu button, press and
  hold the TV button too.
- Hold both buttons until you see the status
  light of the TV start to flash.
- Now release the TV and menu buttons.
- Once you release the buttons, the restart
  would begin.
- The screen would go black for some
  seconds and then the Apple logo would
  display, then you would see the home
  screen.

How to Fix a Bricked Apple TV

If your TV is not responding totally, you may have to connect it to your laptop or desktop and perform a force restore through iTunes. This would only work for the TV HD as the TV 4k does not have a USB-C port.

- Use the USB-C to USB cable to connect your TV to your computer.
- Launch iTunes.
- Choose the Apple TV from the menu.
- Then click on **Restore Apple TV.**

What to do When Having Issues with A Particular App

If you encounter any trouble getting audio or video contents from a specific provider or channel, you may need to contact them. Apple provided a list of contact information for the content providers on their website. You would see the website addresses, phone numbers and email addresses of these services supported on the Apple TV website.

What to do when the Apple TV Refuses to Work
You may need to visit the closest Apple store. You would need the serial number for your device. You can get the serial number in 3 ways.

- For a bricked TV, connect to your Mac or desktop using the USB-C cable and then launch iTunes to view the serial number.

- If your device is able to boot, then go to **settings,** click on **General**, select **About** to get your serial number.

- You can also view the serial number at the bottom of the device, under the FCC information and symbols.

Conclusion

Now that you have known all there is to know in the Apple TV 4K/ HD, I am confident that you would enjoy operating your device.

All relevant areas concerning the usage of the Apple TV from taking out of the box to setup and operations has been carefully outlined and discussed in details to make users more familiar with its operations as well as other information not contained elsewhere.

If you are pleased with the content of this book, don't forget to recommend this book to a friend.

Thank you.

Other Books by the Same Author

- Amazon Echo Dot 3rd Generation User Guide https://amzn.to/2kE3X1T
- Kindle Oasis 3 10th Generation User Guide https://amzn.to/2kGM42w
- Mastering your iPhone XR for beginners, seniors and new iPhone users https://amzn.to/2mgegtc
- Samsung Note 10 and Note 10 Plus User Guide https://amzn.to/2mjBTRG
- Fire TV Stick User Guide https://amzn.to/2kQwTDP

Made in the USA
Columbia, SC
17 July 2020

14070613R00079